42 Seasonal and Sustainable Living Recipes for Home

By: Kelly Johnson

Table of Contents

Spring Salads:

- Strawberry Spinach Salad with Balsamic Vinaigrette
- Asparagus and Pea Salad with Lemon-Dill Dressing
- Radish and Arugula Salad with Avocado-Lime Dressing

Summer Entrees:

- Grilled Vegetable and Quinoa Stuffed Bell Peppers
- Zucchini Noodles with Pesto and Cherry Tomatoes
- Tomato Basil Bruschetta with Grilled Eggplant

Fall Soups:

- Butternut Squash and Apple Soup
- Lentil and Mushroom Soup with Turmeric
- Pumpkin and Kale eStew with White Beans

Winter Comfort Foods:

- Roasted Brussel Sprouts and Sweet Potato Casserole
- Wild Rice and Mushroom Risotto
- Vegan Lentil Shepherd's Pie

Sustainable Seafood:

- Lemon Garlic Baked Salmon with Quinoa
- Grilled Shrimp Tacos with Mango Salsa
- Seared Tuna Poke Bowls with Avocado

Plant-Based Proteins:

- Chickpea and Spinach Coconut Curry
- Black Bean and Corn Stuffed Peppers
- Lentil Walnut Burgers with Tahini Sauce

Breakfast Delights:

- Blueberry Oat Pancakes with Maple Syrup
- Avocado Toast with Radishes and Microgreens
- Chia Seed pudding with Seasonal Fruits

Homemade Snacks:

- Roasted Chickpeas with Smoky Paprika
- Kale Chips with Nutritional Yeast
- Trail Mix with Nuts, Seeds, and Dried Fruits

Preserves and Pickles:

- Strawberry Chia Jam
- Pickled Vegetables with Apple Cider Vinegar
- Tomato Basil Salsa for Canning

Desserts:

- Apple Crisp with Oat Topping
- Vegan Chocolate Avocado Mousse
- Coconut Mango Sorbet

Homemade Beverages:

- Cucumber Mint Infused Water
- Berry and Basil Lemonade
- Iced Green Tea with Honey and Ginger

Fermented Foods:

- Kimchi with Napa Cabbage
- Homemade Sauerkraut with Caraway Seeds
- Pickled Jalapeños for Toppings

Global Flavors:

- Thai-Inspired Pineapple Fried Rice
- Mediterranean Chickpea Salad with Feta
- Mexican Quinoa Stuffed Peppers

Hearty Bowls:

- Soba Noodle Buddha Bowl with Sesame Ginger Dressing
- Moroccan Spiced Couscous Bowl with Roasted Vegetables
- Teriyaki Tofu and Brown Rice Bowl

Spring Salads:

Strawberry Spinach Salad with Balsamic Vinaigrette

Ingredients:

For the Salad:

- 6 cups fresh baby spinach, washed and dried
- 1 pint fresh strawberries, hulled and sliced
- 1/2 cup red onion, thinly sliced
- 1/2 cup feta cheese, crumbled
- 1/2 cup candied pecans or walnuts, chopped

For the Balsamic Vinaigrette:

- 1/4 cup balsamic vinegar
- 1/3 cup extra virgin olive oil
- 1 tablespoon Dijon mustard
- 1 clove garlic, minced
- 1 teaspoon honey or maple syrup (optional for sweetness)
- Salt and pepper to taste

Instructions:

Prepare the Salad:
- In a large salad bowl, combine the fresh baby spinach, sliced strawberries, red onion, crumbled feta cheese, and chopped candied pecans or walnuts.

Make the Balsamic Vinaigrette:
- In a small bowl or jar, whisk together balsamic vinegar, Dijon mustard, minced garlic, and honey or maple syrup (if using). Gradually drizzle in the olive oil while continuing to whisk until the dressing is well-emulsified. Season with salt and pepper to taste.

Assemble the Salad:
- Drizzle the balsamic vinaigrette over the salad, starting with a few tablespoons, and toss gently to coat the ingredients. Add more dressing as needed, ensuring not to overdress the salad.

Serve:
- Transfer the salad to individual plates or a serving platter. Optionally, garnish with additional feta cheese and candied nuts.

Enjoy:
- Serve immediately and enjoy this refreshing and flavorful Strawberry Spinach Salad with Balsamic Vinaigrette!

Tips:

- Adjust the sweetness of the dressing by adding more or less honey or maple syrup according to your taste preferences.
- For an extra burst of flavor, consider adding some fresh mint leaves or basil to the salad.
- To keep the salad crisp, dress it just before serving.

This salad is not only delicious but also a great representation of using seasonal ingredients. Enjoy your culinary creation!

Asparagus and Pea Salad with Lemon-Dill Dressing

Ingredients:

For the Salad:

- 1 bunch asparagus, trimmed and blanched
- 1 cup fresh or frozen peas, blanched
- 1/4 cup red onion, finely chopped
- 1/4 cup feta cheese, crumbled
- 2 tablespoons fresh dill, chopped
- Salt and pepper to taste

For the Lemon-Dill Dressing:

- 3 tablespoons extra virgin olive oil
- 2 tablespoons fresh lemon juice
- 1 teaspoon Dijon mustard
- 1 clove garlic, minced
- 1 teaspoon honey or maple syrup (optional)
- 1 tablespoon fresh dill, chopped
- Salt and pepper to taste

Instructions:

Prepare the Asparagus and Peas:
- Trim the tough ends from the asparagus and blanch them in boiling water for 2-3 minutes until bright green. Immediately transfer to an ice bath to stop the cooking process. Once cooled, cut the asparagus into bite-sized pieces.
- If using fresh peas, blanch them for 1-2 minutes until tender. If using frozen peas, thaw them or blanch for a brief moment. Drain and set aside.

Make the Lemon-Dill Dressing:
- In a small bowl or jar, whisk together olive oil, lemon juice, Dijon mustard, minced garlic, honey or maple syrup (if using), chopped dill, salt, and pepper. Adjust the seasonings to taste.

Assemble the Salad:
- In a large bowl, combine the blanched asparagus, peas, chopped red onion, crumbled feta cheese, and fresh dill.

Add the Dressing:
- Drizzle the lemon-dill dressing over the salad and toss gently to coat the ingredients evenly.

Chill (Optional):
- If desired, refrigerate the salad for about 30 minutes to allow the flavors to meld.

Serve:
- Transfer the salad to a serving platter or individual plates. Garnish with additional dill if desired.

Enjoy:
- Serve this Asparagus and Pea Salad with Lemon-Dill Dressing as a refreshing side dish or a light lunch. Enjoy the vibrant flavors of spring!

Tips:

- Adjust the acidity of the dressing by adding more or less lemon juice according to your preference.
- Feel free to customize the salad by adding other fresh herbs like mint or parsley.
- This salad can be served at room temperature or chilled, depending on your preference.

Radish and Arugula Salad with Avocado-Lime Dressing

Ingredients:

For the Salad:

- 4 cups arugula, washed and dried
- 1 bunch radishes, thinly sliced
- 1/4 cup red onion, thinly sliced
- 1/4 cup goat cheese, crumbled (optional)
- 1/4 cup toasted pumpkin seeds (pepitas)
- Salt and pepper to taste

For the Avocado-Lime Dressing:

- 1 ripe avocado, peeled and pitted
- 1/4 cup fresh lime juice
- 2 tablespoons extra virgin olive oil
- 1 clove garlic, minced
- 1 teaspoon honey or maple syrup
- Salt and pepper to taste

Instructions:

Prepare the Salad:
- In a large salad bowl, combine the arugula, thinly sliced radishes, red onion, crumbled goat cheese (if using), and toasted pumpkin seeds. Toss gently to mix.

Make the Avocado-Lime Dressing:
- In a blender or food processor, combine the ripe avocado, fresh lime juice, olive oil, minced garlic, honey or maple syrup, salt, and pepper. Blend until smooth and creamy.

Dress the Salad:
- Drizzle the avocado-lime dressing over the salad and toss gently until the salad is evenly coated with the dressing.

Season and Garnish:
- Season the salad with salt and pepper to taste. Garnish with additional pumpkin seeds for added crunch.

Serve:

- Transfer the salad to a serving platter or individual plates.

Enjoy:
- Serve the Radish and Arugula Salad with Avocado-Lime Dressing as a refreshing and nutritious side dish or a light lunch. The creamy avocado-lime dressing adds a delightful burst of flavor.

Tips:

- Adjust the sweetness and acidity of the dressing by adding more or less honey or lime juice according to your taste.
- Feel free to customize the salad by adding sliced cucumber or cherry tomatoes for extra freshness.
- To keep the avocado dressing from browning, store it separately and toss it with the salad just before serving.

Summer Entrees:

Grilled Vegetable and Quinoa Stuffed Bell Peppers

Ingredients:

For the Stuffed Bell Peppers:

- 4 large bell peppers, halved and seeds removed
- 1 cup quinoa, rinsed and cooked according to package instructions
- 1 zucchini, diced
- 1 yellow squash, diced
- 1 red onion, diced
- 1 cup cherry tomatoes, halved
- 1 cup corn kernels (fresh or frozen)
- 2 cloves garlic, minced
- 1 teaspoon ground cumin
- 1 teaspoon smoked paprika
- Salt and pepper to taste
- 1 cup shredded mozzarella or your favorite cheese (optional)

For the Avocado-Lime Sauce:

- 1 ripe avocado, peeled and pitted
- 1/4 cup fresh lime juice
- 2 tablespoons fresh cilantro, chopped
- 1/4 cup Greek yogurt (optional for creaminess)
- Salt and pepper to taste

Instructions:

Prepare the Quinoa:
- Rinse the quinoa under cold water. Cook it according to the package instructions. Once cooked, fluff it with a fork and set it aside.

Prepare the Grilled Vegetables:
- In a large bowl, toss the diced zucchini, yellow squash, red onion, cherry tomatoes, and corn with minced garlic, ground cumin, smoked paprika, salt, and pepper.

- Preheat a grill pan or an outdoor grill. Grill the vegetables over medium heat until they are slightly charred and tender, about 8-10 minutes. Remove from the grill and set aside.

Prepare the Avocado-Lime Sauce:

- In a blender or food processor, combine the ripe avocado, fresh lime juice, chopped cilantro, Greek yogurt (if using), salt, and pepper. Blend until smooth and creamy. Adjust the seasoning to your taste.

Assemble the Stuffed Bell Peppers:

- Preheat the oven to 375°F (190°C).
- Place the halved bell peppers in a baking dish.
- In a large bowl, mix the grilled vegetables with the cooked quinoa. If desired, add shredded cheese and mix until combined.
- Stuff each bell pepper half with the quinoa and vegetable mixture, pressing it down gently.

Bake:

- Bake the stuffed bell peppers in the preheated oven for 20-25 minutes or until the peppers are tender and the filling is heated through.

Serve:

- Drizzle the avocado-lime sauce over the stuffed bell peppers just before serving.

Enjoy:

- Serve these Grilled Vegetable and Quinoa Stuffed Bell Peppers as a wholesome and flavorful meal. They are perfect for a light dinner or a nutritious lunch.

Tips:

- Feel free to add your favorite herbs or spices to the quinoa and vegetable mixture for extra flavor.
- Customize the recipe by adding black beans, diced jalapeños, or other vegetables of your choice.
- The Avocado-Lime Sauce can also be served on the side for dipping.

Zucchini Noodles with Pesto and Cherry Tomatoes

Ingredients:

For the Zucchini Noodles:

- 4 medium-sized zucchinis, spiralized into noodles
- 1 tablespoon olive oil
- Salt and pepper to taste

For the Pesto:

- 2 cups fresh basil leaves, packed
- 1/2 cup grated Parmesan cheese
- 1/2 cup pine nuts or walnuts, toasted
- 2 cloves garlic, minced
- 1/2 cup extra virgin olive oil
- Salt and pepper to taste

For Topping:

- 1 cup cherry tomatoes, halved
- Additional grated Parmesan cheese
- Fresh basil leaves for garnish

Instructions:

Prepare the Zucchini Noodles:
- Spiralize the zucchinis into noodles using a spiralizer. If you don't have a spiralizer, you can use a vegetable peeler to create long, thin strips.
- Heat olive oil in a large skillet over medium heat. Add the zucchini noodles and sauté for 2-3 minutes until they are just tender. Season with salt and pepper to taste. Remove from heat and set aside.

Make the Pesto:
- In a food processor, combine basil leaves, grated Parmesan cheese, toasted pine nuts or walnuts, and minced garlic. Pulse until finely chopped.
- With the food processor running, slowly drizzle in the olive oil until the pesto reaches your desired consistency. Season with salt and pepper to taste. Set aside.

Assemble the Dish:
- Toss the zucchini noodles with the prepared pesto until well coated.
- Gently fold in the halved cherry tomatoes.

Serve:
- Divide the zucchini noodles among serving plates.
- Top with additional grated Parmesan cheese and garnish with fresh basil leaves.

Enjoy:
- Serve the Zucchini Noodles with Pesto and Cherry Tomatoes immediately. This dish is light, flavorful, and a perfect way to enjoy the freshness of summer ingredients.

Tips:

- If you prefer warm zucchini noodles, you can briefly heat the pesto in the skillet with the zucchini noodles.
- Customize the pesto by adding a squeeze of lemon juice or a handful of baby spinach for extra freshness.
- Feel free to add grilled chicken, shrimp, or your favorite protein for a heartier meal.

Tomato Basil Bruschetta with Grilled Eggplant

Ingredients:

For the Bruschetta:

- 4 ripe tomatoes, diced
- 1/2 cup fresh basil leaves, chopped
- 2 cloves garlic, minced
- 1/4 cup red onion, finely chopped
- 2 tablespoons balsamic vinegar
- 3 tablespoons extra virgin olive oil
- Salt and pepper to taste

For the Grilled Eggplant:

- 1 large eggplant, sliced into 1/2-inch rounds
- 2 tablespoons olive oil
- Salt and pepper to taste

For Serving:

- Baguette or crusty bread, sliced
- Balsamic glaze (optional)

Instructions:

Prepare the Bruschetta:
- In a bowl, combine the diced tomatoes, chopped basil, minced garlic, finely chopped red onion, balsamic vinegar, and extra virgin olive oil.
- Season the mixture with salt and pepper to taste. Allow it to marinate for at least 15-20 minutes to let the flavors meld.

Grill the Eggplant:
- Preheat the grill or grill pan over medium-high heat.
- Brush the eggplant slices with olive oil and season with salt and pepper.
- Grill the eggplant slices for 2-3 minutes per side or until they have nice grill marks and are tender. Remove from the grill and set aside.

Assemble the Bruschetta:
- Toast the baguette or crusty bread slices.
- Place a grilled eggplant slice on each toasted bread slice.
- Spoon the tomato basil bruschetta mixture generously over the grilled eggplant.

Optional:
- Drizzle with balsamic glaze for an extra burst of flavor.

Serve:
- Arrange the Tomato Basil Bruschetta with Grilled Eggplant on a serving platter.

Enjoy:
- Serve immediately as a delightful appetizer or light meal. The combination of fresh tomatoes, basil, and grilled eggplant creates a delicious and satisfying dish.

Tips:

- You can also add a sprinkle of crumbled feta or goat cheese on top for an extra layer of flavor.
- If you don't have a grill, you can use a grill pan on the stovetop or broil the eggplant slices in the oven until tender.
- Adjust the quantities of ingredients based on your preferences and the number of servings you need.

Fall Soups:

Butternut Squash and Apple Soup

Ingredients:

- 1 medium-sized butternut squash, peeled, seeded, and cubed
- 2 apples, peeled, cored, and chopped (use sweet varieties like Honeycrisp or Fuji)
- 1 onion, chopped
- 2 carrots, peeled and chopped
- 2 cloves garlic, minced
- 4 cups vegetable broth
- 1 teaspoon ground cinnamon
- 1/2 teaspoon ground nutmeg
- 1/2 teaspoon ground ginger
- Salt and pepper to taste
- 2 tablespoons olive oil
- 1 cup unsweetened almond milk or coconut milk (optional, for creaminess)
- Chopped fresh parsley or chives for garnish

Instructions:

Preheat the Oven:
- Preheat the oven to 400°F (200°C).

Roast Butternut Squash and Apples:
- In a large baking sheet, toss the cubed butternut squash, chopped apples, onion, carrots, and minced garlic with olive oil until evenly coated.
- Sprinkle with salt, pepper, ground cinnamon, ground nutmeg, and ground ginger. Toss again to ensure even seasoning.
- Roast in the preheated oven for about 30-40 minutes or until the vegetables are tender and lightly caramelized.

Blend the Soup:
- Transfer the roasted vegetables to a blender or use an immersion blender directly in the pot.
- Add vegetable broth and blend until smooth. You may need to do this in batches if using a traditional blender.

Heat the Soup:

- Pour the blended mixture into a pot. If the soup is too thick, add more vegetable broth to reach your desired consistency.
- Heat the soup over medium heat until warmed through.

Adjust Seasoning:
- Taste the soup and adjust the seasoning, adding more salt, pepper, or spices if needed.

Optional Creaminess:
- For added creaminess, stir in almond milk or coconut milk. Adjust the quantity based on your preference.

Serve:
- Ladle the Butternut Squash and Apple Soup into bowls.

Garnish:
- Garnish with chopped fresh parsley or chives.

Enjoy:
- Serve this warm and comforting soup as a starter or a light meal. The combination of butternut squash and apples provides a delightful sweetness and depth of flavor.

Tips:

- You can customize the level of sweetness by choosing different varieties of apples.
- If you prefer a smoother soup, you can strain it through a fine mesh sieve to remove any remaining solids.
- Consider adding a dash of cayenne pepper or a dollop of Greek yogurt for a hint of heat or creaminess, respectively.

Lentil and Mushroom Soup with Turmeric

Ingredients:

- 1 cup dry brown lentils, rinsed and drained
- 8 oz (about 227g) mushrooms, sliced (cremini or white mushrooms work well)
- 1 large onion, finely chopped
- 3 carrots, peeled and diced
- 3 celery stalks, diced
- 3 cloves garlic, minced
- 1 teaspoon ground turmeric
- 1 teaspoon ground cumin
- 1 teaspoon paprika
- 1/2 teaspoon ground coriander
- 1/4 teaspoon cayenne pepper (adjust to taste, for heat)
- 6 cups vegetable broth
- 1 can (14 oz) diced tomatoes
- 2 bay leaves
- Salt and pepper to taste
- 2 tablespoons olive oil
- Fresh parsley, chopped (for garnish)

Instructions:

Sauté Vegetables:
- In a large pot, heat olive oil over medium heat. Add chopped onions, carrots, celery, and minced garlic. Sauté until the vegetables are softened, about 5-7 minutes.

Add Mushrooms and Spices:
- Add sliced mushrooms to the pot and cook for an additional 5 minutes until they release their moisture and begin to brown.
- Stir in ground turmeric, cumin, paprika, ground coriander, and cayenne pepper. Sauté for 1-2 minutes until the spices are fragrant.

Combine Lentils and Broth:
- Add rinsed lentils, vegetable broth, diced tomatoes (with their juice), and bay leaves to the pot. Bring the mixture to a boil.

Simmer:
- Reduce heat to low, cover the pot, and let the soup simmer for about 25-30 minutes or until the lentils are tender.

Season and Adjust:
- Season the soup with salt and pepper to taste. Adjust the seasoning and spice levels according to your preference.

Serve:
- Remove the bay leaves. Ladle the Lentil and Mushroom Soup into bowls.

Garnish:
- Garnish each serving with fresh chopped parsley.

Enjoy:
- Serve this hearty and nutritious Lentil and Mushroom Soup with Turmeric as a comforting meal. The turmeric adds not only a vibrant color but also anti-inflammatory properties to the dish.

Tips:

- Feel free to add a splash of lemon juice or vinegar just before serving to brighten up the flavors.
- If you prefer a creamier texture, you can blend a portion of the soup with an immersion blender and then mix it back into the pot.
- Serve the soup with a side of crusty bread or whole grain crackers for a complete meal.

Pumpkin and Kale eStew with White Beans

Ingredients:

- 2 tablespoons olive oil
- 1 large onion, diced
- 3 cloves garlic, minced
- 1 teaspoon ground cumin
- 1 teaspoon ground coriander
- 1/2 teaspoon smoked paprika
- 1/4 teaspoon red pepper flakes (optional, for heat)
- 1 can (15 oz) pumpkin puree
- 4 cups vegetable broth
- 1 can (15 oz) white beans (cannellini or great northern), drained and rinsed
- 4 cups kale, stems removed and chopped
- Salt and pepper to taste
- Juice of 1 lemon
- Fresh parsley, chopped (for garnish)

Instructions:

Sauté Aromatics:
- In a large pot, heat olive oil over medium heat. Add diced onions and sauté until softened, about 5 minutes. Add minced garlic and sauté for an additional 1-2 minutes until fragrant.

Add Spices and Pumpkin:
- Stir in ground cumin, ground coriander, smoked paprika, and red pepper flakes (if using). Cook for 1-2 minutes to toast the spices.
- Add pumpkin puree to the pot and mix well with the spices and aromatics.

Pour in Broth and Add White Beans:
- Pour in vegetable broth and add drained white beans to the pot. Stir to combine.

Simmer:
- Bring the mixture to a simmer and let it cook for about 15-20 minutes, allowing the flavors to meld.

Add Kale:
- Add chopped kale to the pot and let it simmer for an additional 5-7 minutes until the kale is wilted and tender.

Season and Finish:

- Season the stew with salt and pepper to taste. Squeeze the juice of one lemon into the pot, adjusting the acidity to your liking.

Serve:
- Ladle the Pumpkin and Kale Stew with White Beans into bowls.

Garnish:
- Garnish with fresh chopped parsley.

Enjoy:
- Serve this hearty and nutritious stew as a comforting meal, especially during the fall and winter seasons. The combination of pumpkin, kale, and white beans provides a delicious and satisfying flavor profile.

Tips:

- Customize the level of spiciness by adjusting the amount of red pepper flakes.
- Feel free to add other vegetables like carrots or celery for extra texture and flavor.
- Serve the stew over cooked quinoa, rice, or with a side of crusty bread for a complete meal.

Winter Comfort Foods:

Roasted Brussel Sprouts and Sweet Potato Casserole

Ingredients:

For the Roasted Vegetables:

- 1 pound Brussels sprouts, trimmed and halved
- 2 large sweet potatoes, peeled and diced into 1-inch cubes
- 3 tablespoons olive oil
- 2 cloves garlic, minced
- Salt and pepper to taste

For the Casserole:

- 1 cup grated Parmesan cheese
- 1 cup breadcrumbs (gluten-free if needed)
- 1/2 cup chopped pecans or walnuts
- 1/4 cup melted butter or olive oil
- 1 teaspoon dried thyme
- 1/2 teaspoon smoked paprika
- 1/2 teaspoon ground cinnamon
- Salt and pepper to taste

Instructions:

Preheat the Oven:
- Preheat your oven to 400°F (200°C).

Roast the Vegetables:
- In a large bowl, toss the halved Brussels sprouts and diced sweet potatoes with olive oil, minced garlic, salt, and pepper until well coated.
- Spread the vegetables in a single layer on a baking sheet. Roast in the preheated oven for 25-30 minutes or until they are golden brown and tender, stirring halfway through.

Prepare the Casserole Topping:

- In a bowl, mix together grated Parmesan cheese, breadcrumbs, chopped pecans or walnuts, melted butter or olive oil, dried thyme, smoked paprika, ground cinnamon, salt, and pepper.

Assemble the Casserole:
- Once the roasted vegetables are done, transfer them to a baking dish.
- Sprinkle the casserole topping evenly over the roasted Brussels sprouts and sweet potatoes.

Bake:
- Bake the casserole in the oven for an additional 15-20 minutes or until the topping is golden and crispy.

Serve:
- Remove from the oven and let it cool for a few minutes before serving.

Enjoy:
- Serve this Roasted Brussels Sprouts and Sweet Potato Casserole as a flavorful and wholesome side dish for your holiday gatherings or as part of a cozy family meal.

Tips:

- Adjust the seasoning in the topping to suit your taste preferences.
- Feel free to add a drizzle of balsamic glaze or maple syrup over the casserole just before serving for extra sweetness.
- You can make the casserole ahead of time and reheat it in the oven before serving.

Wild Rice and Mushroom Risotto

Ingredients:

- 1 cup wild rice
- 4 cups vegetable broth
- 2 tablespoons olive oil
- 1 large onion, finely chopped
- 2 cloves garlic, minced
- 8 oz (about 227g) mushrooms (button or cremini), sliced
- 1 cup Arborio rice
- 1/2 cup dry white wine (optional)
- 1 teaspoon dried thyme
- 1/2 teaspoon dried rosemary
- Salt and black pepper to taste
- 1/2 cup grated Parmesan cheese
- 2 tablespoons unsalted butter
- Fresh parsley, chopped (for garnish)

Instructions:

Prepare Wild Rice:
- In a separate pot, cook the wild rice according to package instructions, using vegetable broth instead of water for added flavor. This typically takes around 45-50 minutes. Set aside.

Sauté Onions and Garlic:
- In a large skillet or saucepan, heat olive oil over medium heat. Add chopped onions and sauté until they become translucent, about 5 minutes. Add minced garlic and cook for an additional 1-2 minutes.

Cook Mushrooms:
- Add sliced mushrooms to the skillet and cook until they release their moisture and become golden brown, about 6-8 minutes.

Toast Arborio Rice:
- Stir in Arborio rice and cook for 2-3 minutes, allowing the rice to toast slightly.

Deglaze with Wine (Optional):
- Pour in the white wine (if using) to deglaze the pan, stirring until most of the liquid evaporates.

Add Herbs and Seasoning:

- Stir in dried thyme, dried rosemary, salt, and black pepper. Mix well.

Add Vegetable Broth:
- Begin adding the vegetable broth, one ladle at a time, stirring continuously. Allow the liquid to be absorbed before adding the next ladle. Continue this process until the Arborio rice is creamy and cooked to al dente, which usually takes about 18-20 minutes.

Combine with Wild Rice:
- Once the Arborio rice is almost cooked, stir in the cooked wild rice.

Finish and Garnish:
- Once the rice mixture reaches a creamy consistency, stir in grated Parmesan cheese and unsalted butter. Adjust salt and pepper to taste.

Serve:
- Remove from heat and let the risotto sit for a minute. Garnish with fresh chopped parsley.

Enjoy:
- Serve this rich and savory Wild Rice and Mushroom Risotto immediately as a delicious main course or a side dish.

Tips:

- Feel free to experiment with different mushroom varieties for added depth of flavor.
- If you prefer a dairy-free option, you can skip the Parmesan cheese and butter or use plant-based alternatives.
- Use a good-quality vegetable broth to enhance the overall flavor of the risotto.

Vegan Lentil Shepherd's Pie

Ingredients:

For the Lentil Filling:

- 1 cup dry green or brown lentils, rinsed
- 3 cups vegetable broth
- 1 tablespoon olive oil
- 1 onion, finely chopped
- 2 carrots, diced
- 2 celery stalks, diced
- 3 cloves garlic, minced
- 1 teaspoon dried thyme
- 1 teaspoon dried rosemary
- 1 teaspoon smoked paprika
- 1 can (14 oz) diced tomatoes, drained
- Salt and black pepper to taste

For the Mashed Potato Topping:

- 4 large potatoes, peeled and diced
- 1/2 cup unsweetened almond milk or any plant-based milk
- 2 tablespoons vegan butter
- Salt and black pepper to taste

For Assembly:

- Fresh parsley, chopped (for garnish)

Instructions:

Prepare Lentil Filling:
- In a saucepan, combine lentils and vegetable broth. Bring to a boil, then reduce heat, cover, and simmer until lentils are tender but not mushy, about 20-25 minutes.

Sauté Vegetables:

- In a large skillet, heat olive oil over medium heat. Add chopped onion, carrots, and celery. Sauté until vegetables are softened, about 8-10 minutes.

Add Aromatics and Lentils:
- Add minced garlic, dried thyme, dried rosemary, and smoked paprika to the skillet. Stir and cook for 1-2 minutes. Add the cooked lentils and diced tomatoes. Season with salt and black pepper. Stir well and let it simmer for 5-7 minutes.

Prepare Mashed Potato Topping:
- While the lentil mixture is simmering, boil the diced potatoes in a large pot of salted water until tender. Drain the potatoes and mash them with almond milk, vegan butter, salt, and black pepper until smooth.

Assemble and Bake:
- Preheat the oven to 400°F (200°C).
- Transfer the lentil filling to a baking dish and spread it evenly.
- Top the lentil mixture with the mashed potatoes, spreading them out with a spatula.

Bake:
- Place the baking dish in the preheated oven and bake for 20-25 minutes or until the top is golden brown.

Garnish and Serve:
- Remove from the oven and let it cool for a few minutes. Garnish with chopped fresh parsley before serving.

Enjoy:
- Serve this Vegan Lentil Shepherd's Pie as a hearty and satisfying plant-based meal.

Tips:

- Feel free to add frozen peas or corn to the lentil filling for extra color and texture.
- You can customize the mashed potato topping by adding garlic powder or nutritional yeast for additional flavor.
- Make sure the lentils are well-cooked but still hold their shape to maintain a hearty texture in the filling.

Sustainable Seafood:

Lemon Garlic Baked Salmon with Quinoa

Ingredients:

For the Lemon Garlic Baked Salmon:

- 4 salmon fillets
- 2 tablespoons olive oil
- 3 cloves garlic, minced
- Zest of 1 lemon
- Juice of 1 lemon
- 1 teaspoon dried oregano
- Salt and black pepper to taste
- Lemon slices for garnish

For the Quinoa:

- 1 cup quinoa, rinsed
- 2 cups vegetable broth or water
- 1 tablespoon olive oil
- Salt to taste

For Garnish:

- Fresh parsley, chopped
- Lemon wedges

Instructions:

Preheat the Oven:
- Preheat your oven to 400°F (200°C).

Prepare the Salmon:
- Place the salmon fillets on a baking sheet lined with parchment paper.
- In a small bowl, mix together olive oil, minced garlic, lemon zest, lemon juice, dried oregano, salt, and black pepper.
- Brush the salmon fillets with the lemon garlic mixture, ensuring they are well-coated. Place lemon slices on top of each fillet.

Bake the Salmon:
- Bake the salmon in the preheated oven for 12-15 minutes or until the salmon flakes easily with a fork and has a golden brown color.

Prepare the Quinoa:
- While the salmon is baking, rinse the quinoa under cold water. In a saucepan, combine quinoa and vegetable broth or water. Bring to a boil.
- Reduce the heat to low, cover, and simmer for 15-20 minutes, or until the quinoa is cooked and the liquid is absorbed.
- Fluff the quinoa with a fork and stir in olive oil. Season with salt to taste.

Serve:
- Divide the cooked quinoa among serving plates.
- Place the baked salmon fillets on top of the quinoa.

Garnish:
- Garnish the dish with chopped fresh parsley and serve with lemon wedges on the side.

Enjoy:
- Enjoy this Lemon Garlic Baked Salmon with Quinoa as a flavorful and nutritious meal. It's a perfect combination of vibrant flavors and textures.

Tips:

- You can add additional herbs or spices to the lemon garlic marinade, such as fresh chopped dill or parsley.
- Feel free to customize the quinoa with your favorite herbs or vegetables for added variety.
- Serve with steamed vegetables or a side salad for a complete and balanced meal.

Grilled Shrimp Tacos with Mango Salsa

Ingredients:

For the Grilled Shrimp:

- 1 pound large shrimp, peeled and deveined
- 2 tablespoons olive oil
- 2 cloves garlic, minced
- 1 teaspoon chili powder
- 1 teaspoon cumin
- Salt and black pepper to taste
- Juice of 1 lime

For the Mango Salsa:

- 1 ripe mango, peeled and diced
- 1/2 red onion, finely chopped
- 1 jalapeño, seeds removed and finely chopped
- 1/4 cup fresh cilantro, chopped
- Juice of 1 lime
- Salt to taste

For the Tacos:

- 8 small flour or corn tortillas
- Shredded lettuce or cabbage
- Avocado slices
- Greek yogurt or sour cream (optional)
- Lime wedges for serving

Instructions:

Marinate and Grill the Shrimp:
- In a bowl, combine olive oil, minced garlic, chili powder, cumin, salt, black pepper, and lime juice. Add the peeled and deveined shrimp to the marinade, ensuring they are well-coated. Marinate for at least 15-30 minutes.
- Preheat the grill or grill pan over medium-high heat. Thread the marinated shrimp onto skewers.

- Grill the shrimp for 2-3 minutes per side or until they are opaque and cooked through.

Prepare the Mango Salsa:
- In a bowl, combine diced mango, finely chopped red onion, jalapeño, cilantro, lime juice, and salt. Mix well to combine.

Assemble the Tacos:
- Warm the tortillas according to package instructions.
- Assemble the tacos by placing a layer of shredded lettuce or cabbage on each tortilla.
- Add grilled shrimp on top of the lettuce.
- Spoon mango salsa over the shrimp.
- Add avocado slices and a dollop of Greek yogurt or sour cream if desired.

Serve:
- Serve the Grilled Shrimp Tacos with Mango Salsa immediately, with lime wedges on the side.

Enjoy:
- Enjoy these vibrant and flavorful shrimp tacos as a delightful and satisfying meal.

Tips:

- Customize the spice level of the shrimp marinade and salsa by adjusting the amount of chili powder and jalapeño.
- Add other favorite taco toppings such as shredded cheese or a squeeze of hot sauce.
- If using wooden skewers for the shrimp, make sure to soak them in water for about 30 minutes before grilling to prevent them from burning.

Seared Tuna Poke Bowls with Avocado

Ingredients:

For the Seared Tuna:

- 1 pound sushi-grade tuna, cut into bite-sized cubes
- 2 tablespoons soy sauce
- 1 tablespoon sesame oil
- 1 teaspoon rice vinegar
- 1 teaspoon honey or maple syrup
- 1 teaspoon grated fresh ginger
- 1 tablespoon sesame seeds
- 2 green onions, thinly sliced

For the Poke Bowls:

- 2 cups cooked sushi rice or quinoa
- 1 ripe avocado, sliced
- 1 cucumber, julienned
- 1 carrot, julienned
- 1 cup edamame, shelled and steamed
- Radish slices for garnish
- Fresh cilantro or microgreens for garnish
- Lime wedges for serving

Optional Additions:

- Sriracha or spicy mayo for drizzling
- Furikake seasoning for extra flavor

Instructions:

Prepare the Seared Tuna:
- In a bowl, combine soy sauce, sesame oil, rice vinegar, honey or maple syrup, grated ginger, sesame seeds, and sliced green onions. Mix well.

- Add the tuna cubes to the marinade, making sure they are well coated. Allow the tuna to marinate for about 15-20 minutes in the refrigerator.
- In a hot skillet or grill pan, sear the marinated tuna for about 30 seconds to 1 minute on each side, keeping the inside rare. Remove from heat.

Assemble the Poke Bowls:
- Divide the cooked sushi rice or quinoa among serving bowls.
- Arrange the seared tuna on top of the rice.
- Add sliced avocado, julienned cucumber, julienned carrot, and steamed edamame to each bowl.
- Garnish with radish slices, fresh cilantro or microgreens.

Drizzle and Serve:
- Drizzle the poke bowls with additional soy sauce, sesame oil, or your favorite sauce.
- Optionally, add a drizzle of Sriracha or spicy mayo for some heat.

Garnish and Serve:
- Garnish with extra sesame seeds and a wedge of lime on the side.

Enjoy:
- Serve these Seared Tuna Poke Bowls with Avocado immediately, offering a burst of flavors and textures in every bite.

Tips:

- Be sure to use sushi-grade tuna for the seared tuna to ensure freshness and safety.
- Customize the bowl with your favorite vegetables or toppings.
- If you enjoy spice, consider adding a sprinkle of Furikake seasoning or extra chili flakes.

Plant-Based Proteins:

Chickpea and Spinach Coconut Curry

Ingredients:

- 2 tablespoons coconut oil
- 1 large onion, finely chopped
- 3 cloves garlic, minced
- 1 tablespoon ginger, grated
- 1 tablespoon curry powder
- 1 teaspoon ground cumin
- 1 teaspoon ground coriander
- 1/2 teaspoon turmeric
- 1/4 teaspoon cayenne pepper (adjust to taste)
- 1 can (15 oz) chickpeas, drained and rinsed
- 1 can (14 oz) diced tomatoes
- 1 can (14 oz) coconut milk
- 4 cups fresh spinach, washed and chopped
- Salt and black pepper to taste
- Fresh cilantro, chopped (for garnish)
- Cooked rice or naan bread (for serving)

Instructions:

Sauté Aromatics:
- In a large skillet or pot, heat coconut oil over medium heat. Add chopped onion and cook until softened, about 3-4 minutes.

Add Spices:
- Add minced garlic and grated ginger to the onions. Sauté for an additional 1-2 minutes until fragrant.
- Stir in curry powder, ground cumin, ground coriander, turmeric, and cayenne pepper. Cook for another 1-2 minutes to toast the spices.

Combine Chickpeas and Tomatoes:
- Add drained chickpeas to the skillet and stir to coat them in the spice mixture.
- Pour in diced tomatoes with their juice. Stir well to combine.

Simmer with Coconut Milk:

- Pour in the coconut milk and bring the mixture to a simmer. Let it cook for 10-15 minutes, allowing the flavors to meld and the sauce to thicken slightly.

Add Spinach:
- Stir in the chopped fresh spinach. Let it cook for an additional 2-3 minutes until the spinach wilts into the curry.

Season:
- Season the curry with salt and black pepper to taste. Adjust the spices if needed.

Serve:
- Serve the Chickpea and Spinach Coconut Curry over cooked rice or with naan bread.

Garnish:
- Garnish with fresh chopped cilantro before serving.

Enjoy:
- Enjoy this flavorful and comforting Chickpea and Spinach Coconut Curry as a delicious vegan or vegetarian meal.

Tips:

- Customize the spice levels by adjusting the amount of cayenne pepper or adding fresh chili for more heat.
- You can add other vegetables like bell peppers or sweet potatoes for added texture and flavor.
- For extra richness, you can stir in a couple of tablespoons of coconut cream just before serving.

Black Bean and Corn Stuffed Peppers

Ingredients:

- 4 large bell peppers, halved and seeds removed
- 1 cup cooked quinoa or rice
- 1 can (15 oz) black beans, drained and rinsed
- 1 cup corn kernels (fresh, frozen, or canned)
- 1 cup diced tomatoes
- 1 cup diced red onion
- 1 cup shredded Mexican blend cheese
- 2 cloves garlic, minced
- 1 teaspoon ground cumin
- 1 teaspoon chili powder
- Salt and black pepper to taste
- Olive oil for drizzling
- Fresh cilantro, chopped (for garnish)
- Avocado slices (for serving, optional)
- Lime wedges (for serving, optional)

Instructions:

Preheat the Oven:
- Preheat your oven to 375°F (190°C).

Prepare the Peppers:
- Cut the bell peppers in half lengthwise, removing the seeds and membranes. Place them in a baking dish.

Prepare the Filling:
- In a large mixing bowl, combine cooked quinoa or rice, black beans, corn, diced tomatoes, red onion, shredded cheese, minced garlic, ground cumin, chili powder, salt, and black pepper. Mix well.

Stuff the Peppers:
- Spoon the filling mixture into each pepper half, pressing it down gently.

Bake:
- Drizzle a bit of olive oil over the stuffed peppers. Cover the baking dish with foil.
- Bake in the preheated oven for 25-30 minutes, or until the peppers are tender.

Broil (Optional):
- If you want to brown the cheese on top, remove the foil and broil for an additional 2-3 minutes until the cheese is bubbly and golden.

Garnish and Serve:
- Remove from the oven and let the stuffed peppers cool slightly.
- Garnish with fresh chopped cilantro. Serve with avocado slices and lime wedges if desired.

Enjoy:
- Enjoy these Black Bean and Corn Stuffed Peppers as a satisfying and flavorful vegetarian meal.

Tips:

- Feel free to add your favorite toppings such as salsa, guacamole, or a dollop of Greek yogurt.
- You can customize the filling with additional vegetables like diced zucchini or bell peppers for extra color and texture.
- Make it vegan by omitting the cheese or using a plant-based cheese alternative.

Lentil Walnut Burgers with Tahini Sauce

Ingredients:

For the Lentil Walnut Burgers:

- 1 cup dry green or brown lentils, cooked and drained
- 1 cup walnuts, finely chopped
- 1/2 cup breadcrumbs (regular or gluten-free)
- 1/2 cup finely diced onion
- 2 cloves garlic, minced
- 1 teaspoon ground cumin
- 1 teaspoon ground coriander
- 1 teaspoon smoked paprika
- 1/2 teaspoon cayenne pepper (adjust to taste)
- Salt and black pepper to taste
- 1 tablespoon soy sauce or tamari
- 2 tablespoons tomato paste
- 1 tablespoon Dijon mustard
- 2 tablespoons olive oil (for cooking)
- Burger buns and your favorite toppings for serving

For the Tahini Sauce:

- 1/2 cup tahini
- 2 tablespoons lemon juice
- 2 tablespoons water
- 1 clove garlic, minced
- Salt to taste

Instructions:

Prepare Lentil Walnut Burger Patties:
- In a large bowl, combine cooked lentils, chopped walnuts, breadcrumbs, diced onion, minced garlic, ground cumin, ground coriander, smoked paprika, cayenne pepper, salt, and black pepper.
- Add soy sauce or tamari, tomato paste, and Dijon mustard. Mix until well combined.
- Form the mixture into burger patties.

Cook the Burger Patties:
- In a large skillet, heat olive oil over medium heat. Cook the burger patties for 4-5 minutes on each side or until they are golden brown and cooked through.

Prepare Tahini Sauce:
- In a small bowl, whisk together tahini, lemon juice, water, minced garlic, and salt. Adjust the consistency by adding more water if needed.

Assemble the Burgers:
- Toast the burger buns if desired.
- Place a lentil walnut burger patty on each bun and top with your favorite toppings.
- Drizzle tahini sauce over the burger patties.

Serve:
- Serve these Lentil Walnut Burgers with Tahini Sauce immediately, accompanied by a side salad or your favorite side dishes.

Tips:

- Customize the burger toppings with lettuce, tomato, red onion, avocado, or pickles.
- Experiment with different spices and herbs in the burger patties to suit your taste preferences.
- These burgers can also be grilled or baked in the oven for a different cooking method. Adjust the cooking time accordingly.

Breakfast Delights:

Blueberry Oat Pancakes with Maple Syrup

Ingredients:

- 1 cup old-fashioned oats
- 1 cup all-purpose flour
- 2 tablespoons sugar
- 1 tablespoon baking powder
- 1/2 teaspoon baking soda
- 1/4 teaspoon salt
- 1 cup buttermilk
- 1/2 cup milk
- 2 large eggs
- 1/4 cup melted butter or oil
- 1 teaspoon vanilla extract
- 1 cup fresh or frozen blueberries
- Maple syrup for serving
- Additional blueberries and sliced bananas for garnish (optional)

Instructions:

Prepare the Pancake Batter:
- In a blender or food processor, pulse the old-fashioned oats until they resemble a coarse flour.
- In a large mixing bowl, combine the oat flour, all-purpose flour, sugar, baking powder, baking soda, and salt.
- In a separate bowl, whisk together buttermilk, milk, eggs, melted butter or oil, and vanilla extract.
- Pour the wet ingredients into the dry ingredients and stir until just combined. Be careful not to overmix; a few lumps are okay.

Add Blueberries:
- Gently fold in the blueberries into the pancake batter.

Cook the Pancakes:
- Heat a griddle or non-stick skillet over medium heat. Lightly grease with butter or oil.

- Pour 1/4 cup of batter onto the griddle for each pancake. Cook until bubbles form on the surface, then flip and cook the other side until golden brown.
- Repeat until all the batter is used, keeping the cooked pancakes warm in a low oven if needed.

Serve:
- Stack the Blueberry Oat Pancakes on a plate. Drizzle with maple syrup.

Garnish (Optional):
- Garnish with additional blueberries and sliced bananas if desired.

Enjoy:
- Enjoy these delicious and wholesome Blueberry Oat Pancakes for a delightful breakfast treat!

Tips:

- To make oat flour at home, simply grind old-fashioned oats in a blender or food processor until finely ground.
- If you don't have buttermilk, you can make a substitute by adding 1 tablespoon of white vinegar or lemon juice to a cup of milk and letting it sit for 5 minutes.
- Feel free to customize these pancakes by adding a sprinkle of cinnamon or nutmeg to the batter for extra flavor.

Avocado Toast with Radishes and Microgreens

Ingredients:

- 2 slices of whole-grain bread (or bread of your choice)
- 1 ripe avocado
- 4-6 radishes, thinly sliced
- Handful of microgreens (such as pea shoots or sunflower sprouts)
- Lemon juice
- Salt and pepper to taste
- Red pepper flakes (optional, for a bit of heat)

Instructions:

Toast the Bread:
- Toast the slices of bread to your desired level of crispiness.

Prepare the Avocado:
- While the bread is toasting, cut the avocado in half, remove the pit, and scoop the flesh into a bowl.
- Mash the avocado with a fork and add a squeeze of lemon juice. Season with salt and pepper to taste.

Assemble the Avocado Toast:
- Spread the mashed avocado evenly over each slice of toasted bread.
- Arrange the thinly sliced radishes on top of the avocado.
- Sprinkle microgreens over the radishes.

Season and Garnish:
- Drizzle a bit more lemon juice over the assembled toasts for brightness.
- If you like a bit of heat, sprinkle red pepper flakes on top.

Serve:
- Serve the Avocado Toast with Radishes and Microgreens immediately.

Enjoy:
- Enjoy this nutritious and flavorful avocado toast as a quick and satisfying breakfast or snack.

Tips:

- Experiment with different types of bread, such as sourdough, whole-grain, or multigrain, to add variety to your avocado toast.

- You can customize the toppings by adding a poached or fried egg, cherry tomatoes, or a drizzle of balsamic glaze.
- Feel free to explore other microgreen varieties based on availability and personal preference.

Chia Seed pudding with Seasonal Fruits

Ingredients:

For the Chia Seed Pudding:

- 1/4 cup chia seeds
- 1 cup almond milk (or any milk of your choice)
- 1 tablespoon maple syrup or honey
- 1/2 teaspoon vanilla extract

For the Toppings:

- Seasonal fruits (e.g., berries, sliced kiwi, mango, or any fruits in season)
- Nuts (e.g., sliced almonds or chopped walnuts)
- Fresh mint leaves (for garnish)

Instructions:

Prepare the Chia Seed Pudding:
- In a bowl, combine chia seeds, almond milk, maple syrup or honey, and vanilla extract.
- Stir the mixture well to ensure the chia seeds are evenly distributed. Let it sit for a few minutes.
- Stir again after a few minutes to prevent clumping, then cover and refrigerate for at least 2-3 hours or overnight. The chia seeds will absorb the liquid and create a pudding-like consistency.

Assemble the Chia Seed Pudding:
- Once the chia pudding has set, give it a good stir to break up any clumps.
- Spoon the chia pudding into serving glasses or bowls.

Add Seasonal Fruits and Toppings:
- Top the chia pudding with an assortment of seasonal fruits. Use a variety of colors and textures for a visually appealing dish.
- Sprinkle nuts, such as sliced almonds or chopped walnuts, over the fruits.

Garnish and Serve:
- Garnish the chia seed pudding with fresh mint leaves for a burst of freshness.

- Serve immediately and enjoy your Chia Seed Pudding with Seasonal Fruits.

Tips:

- Experiment with different types of milk, such as coconut milk or soy milk, to vary the flavor of the chia seed pudding.
- Adjust the sweetness by adding more or less maple syrup or honey according to your taste preferences.
- Get creative with the toppings, incorporating granola, coconut flakes, or a dollop of yogurt for additional texture and flavor.

Homemade Snacks:

Roasted Chickpeas with Smoky Paprika

Ingredients:

- 2 cans (15 oz each) chickpeas, drained, rinsed, and patted dry
- 2 tablespoons olive oil
- 1 teaspoon smoky paprika
- 1/2 teaspoon garlic powder
- 1/2 teaspoon onion powder
- 1/2 teaspoon cumin
- 1/2 teaspoon salt (adjust to taste)
- 1/4 teaspoon black pepper
- Optional: cayenne pepper for a bit of heat

Instructions:

Preheat the Oven:
- Preheat your oven to 400°F (200°C).

Prepare the Chickpeas:
- Drain and rinse the chickpeas. Pat them dry with a paper towel to remove excess moisture.

Season the Chickpeas:
- In a bowl, toss the chickpeas with olive oil, smoky paprika, garlic powder, onion powder, cumin, salt, black pepper, and cayenne pepper if you like it spicy. Ensure the chickpeas are well-coated with the seasoning.

Roast in the Oven:
- Spread the seasoned chickpeas in a single layer on a baking sheet.
- Roast in the preheated oven for 25-30 minutes or until the chickpeas are golden brown and crispy. Shake the pan or stir the chickpeas halfway through the cooking time for even roasting.

Cool and Serve:
- Allow the roasted chickpeas to cool for a few minutes. They will continue to crisp up as they cool.

Enjoy:
- Enjoy the smoky paprika roasted chickpeas as a snack on their own or as a crunchy topping for salads and soups.

Tips:

- Experiment with different spice combinations, such as adding a pinch of smoked sea salt or a touch of lemon zest for extra flavor.
- Customize the level of spiciness by adjusting the amount of cayenne pepper or adding your favorite hot sauce after roasting.
- Make a larger batch and store the roasted chickpeas in an airtight container for a convenient and healthy snack option.

Kale Chips with Nutritional Yeast

Ingredients:

- 1 bunch of kale, stems removed and leaves torn into bite-sized pieces
- 2 tablespoons olive oil
- 2 tablespoons nutritional yeast
- 1/2 teaspoon garlic powder
- 1/2 teaspoon onion powder
- 1/4 teaspoon smoked paprika (optional, for extra flavor)
- Salt and pepper to taste

Instructions:

Preheat the Oven:
- Preheat your oven to 300°F (150°C).

Prepare the Kale:
- Wash the kale leaves thoroughly and pat them dry using a clean kitchen towel or paper towels. Ensure they are completely dry to achieve crispiness.
- Remove the stems and tear the kale leaves into bite-sized pieces.

Massage with Olive Oil:
- In a large bowl, toss the kale pieces with olive oil, making sure each leaf is coated evenly.

Season the Kale:
- Sprinkle nutritional yeast, garlic powder, onion powder, smoked paprika (if using), salt, and pepper over the kale. Toss the kale again to evenly distribute the seasonings.

Bake the Kale Chips:
- Spread the seasoned kale pieces in a single layer on baking sheets. You may need to use multiple sheets or bake in batches to avoid overcrowding.
- Bake in the preheated oven for 15-20 minutes, or until the edges of the kale are crispy but not burnt. Keep a close eye on them to prevent overcooking.

Cool and Enjoy:
- Allow the kale chips to cool for a few minutes on the baking sheets. They will continue to crisp up as they cool.

Serve:

- Transfer the kale chips to a serving bowl or enjoy them directly from the baking sheets.

Enjoy:
- Enjoy the nutritional yeast kale chips as a crunchy and flavorful snack!

Tips:

- Customize the seasoning by adding your favorite herbs or spices, such as cayenne pepper, paprika, or a squeeze of lemon juice.
- Adjust the quantity of nutritional yeast according to your taste preferences.
- Store any leftover kale chips in an airtight container to maintain their crispiness.

Trail Mix with Nuts, Seeds, and Dried Fruits

Ingredients:

- 1 cup almonds
- 1 cup walnuts
- 1/2 cup pumpkin seeds
- 1/2 cup sunflower seeds
- 1/2 cup cashews
- 1/2 cup dried cranberries
- 1/2 cup raisins
- 1/2 cup dried apricots, chopped
- 1/2 cup dark chocolate chips or chunks
- Optional: 1/2 cup coconut flakes or chips

Instructions:

Prepare Nuts and Seeds:
- If the nuts are raw, you can roast them for added flavor. Preheat the oven to 350°F (175°C), spread the nuts on a baking sheet, and roast for about 8-10 minutes or until they become fragrant. Allow them to cool completely.

Combine Ingredients:
- In a large bowl, combine the almonds, walnuts, pumpkin seeds, sunflower seeds, cashews, dried cranberries, raisins, dried apricots, and dark chocolate chips. Add coconut flakes if you're using them.

Mix Thoroughly:
- Toss all the ingredients together until they are evenly distributed.

Store:
- Transfer your trail mix to an airtight container or portion them into individual snack-sized bags for convenience.

Enjoy:
- Enjoy your homemade trail mix as a nutritious and energy-boosting snack for hikes, work, or whenever you need a quick pick-me-up.

Tips:

- Feel free to experiment with different nuts and seeds, such as pecans, pistachios, or chia seeds, to create your preferred mix.

- Choose unsweetened and unsalted nuts whenever possible to control the amount of sugar and sodium in your trail mix.
- Add dried fruits that you enjoy, like dried mango, pineapple, or cherries, for a burst of natural sweetness.
- Customize the trail mix to cater to any dietary preferences or restrictions you may have.

Preserves and Pickles:

Strawberry Chia Jam

Ingredients:

- 2 cups fresh strawberries, hulled and chopped
- 2-3 tablespoons maple syrup or honey (adjust according to sweetness preference)
- 2 tablespoons chia seeds
- 1 tablespoon lemon juice
- 1 teaspoon vanilla extract (optional)

Instructions:

Prepare the Strawberries:
- Wash, hull, and chop the fresh strawberries.

Cook the Strawberries:
- In a saucepan over medium heat, add the chopped strawberries and maple syrup or honey. Cook the strawberries until they start to break down and release their juices, stirring occasionally. This usually takes about 5-7 minutes.

Mash the Strawberries:
- Using a potato masher or the back of a spoon, mash the strawberries to your desired consistency. Leave some chunks for texture.

Add Chia Seeds:
- Stir in the chia seeds. Continue to cook for an additional 5-7 minutes, allowing the chia seeds to absorb the liquid and thicken the jam.

Add Lemon Juice and Vanilla Extract:
- Add lemon juice to enhance the flavor and give the jam a bit of brightness. If desired, add vanilla extract for extra depth of flavor.

Adjust Sweetness:
- Taste the jam and adjust the sweetness by adding more maple syrup or honey if needed.

Cool and Store:
- Remove the saucepan from heat and let the strawberry chia jam cool to room temperature. As it cools, it will continue to thicken.

- Transfer the jam to a jar or airtight container and refrigerate for at least 2 hours or overnight to allow it to fully set.

Enjoy:
- Use your strawberry chia jam on toast, yogurt, pancakes, or as a topping for desserts. Enjoy this delicious and healthier alternative to traditional jam!

Tips:

- Feel free to mix in other berries like blueberries or raspberries for a mixed berry chia jam.
- Experiment with different sweeteners or a combination of sweeteners to suit your taste preferences.
- Adjust the consistency by adding more or fewer chia seeds based on your desired thickness.

Pickled Vegetables with Apple Cider Vinegar

Ingredients:

- 2 cups mixed vegetables (carrots, cucumbers, bell peppers, cauliflower, etc.), thinly sliced or chopped
- 1 cup apple cider vinegar
- 1 cup water
- 2 tablespoons sugar
- 1 tablespoon salt
- 1 teaspoon whole mustard seeds
- 1 teaspoon whole coriander seeds
- 1/2 teaspoon black peppercorns
- 2 cloves garlic, smashed
- Optional: red pepper flakes for added heat

Instructions:

Prepare the Vegetables:
- Wash and thinly slice or chop the vegetables of your choice. Ensure they are cut to a size that allows them to absorb the pickling liquid.

Prepare the Pickling Liquid:
- In a saucepan, combine apple cider vinegar, water, sugar, salt, mustard seeds, coriander seeds, black peppercorns, smashed garlic cloves, and red pepper flakes if using.

Bring to a Boil:
- Bring the mixture to a boil over medium-high heat, stirring occasionally to dissolve the sugar and salt.

Simmer:
- Reduce the heat and let the liquid simmer for about 5 minutes to allow the flavors to meld.

Cool the Pickling Liquid:
- Remove the saucepan from heat and let the pickling liquid cool to room temperature.

Pack the Vegetables:
- Pack the sliced or chopped vegetables into clean, sterile jars or a glass container with a tight-fitting lid.

Pour the Pickling Liquid:

- Pour the cooled pickling liquid over the vegetables, ensuring they are fully submerged. If needed, use a spoon to press down the vegetables and remove any air bubbles.

Refrigerate:
- Seal the jars or container and refrigerate for at least 24 hours to allow the flavors to develop.

Enjoy:
- Your pickled vegetables with apple cider vinegar are ready to be enjoyed! Serve them as a crunchy side, on top of salads, or in sandwiches.

Tips:

- Experiment with different vegetables and herbs to create your favorite pickled combination.
- You can customize the sweetness and acidity by adjusting the sugar and apple cider vinegar amounts.
- These pickled vegetables can be stored in the refrigerator for several weeks.

Tomato Basil Salsa for Canning

Ingredients:

- 10 cups tomatoes, peeled, cored, and chopped
- 2 cups onions, finely chopped
- 1 cup bell peppers (red, green, or a mix), finely chopped
- 4 cloves garlic, minced
- 2 cups fresh basil, chopped
- 1 1/2 cups apple cider vinegar
- 1 cup tomato paste
- 1/2 cup granulated sugar
- 2 teaspoons salt
- 1 teaspoon black pepper
- 1 teaspoon dried oregano
- 1 teaspoon dried thyme
- 1 teaspoon crushed red pepper flakes (optional, for heat)

Instructions:

Prepare the Jars and Lids:
- Sterilize your canning jars and lids according to the manufacturer's instructions.

Prepare the Tomatoes:
- Blanch the tomatoes in boiling water for about 1 minute. Transfer them to an ice bath, and then peel, core, and chop them.

Combine Ingredients:
- In a large pot, combine the chopped tomatoes, onions, bell peppers, garlic, basil, apple cider vinegar, tomato paste, sugar, salt, black pepper, oregano, thyme, and crushed red pepper flakes if using.

Cook the Salsa:
- Bring the mixture to a boil over medium-high heat. Reduce the heat and simmer, stirring frequently, for about 30-40 minutes or until the salsa thickens to your desired consistency.

Check and Adjust Seasoning:
- Taste the salsa and adjust the seasoning if needed. Add more salt, sugar, or vinegar according to your taste preference.

Fill the Jars:

- Ladle the hot salsa into the sterilized jars, leaving about 1/2-inch headspace.

Remove Air Bubbles:
- Run a spatula or wooden stick around the inside edge of the jars to remove any air bubbles.

Wipe Jar Rims and Apply Lids:
- Wipe the rims of the jars with a clean, damp cloth to remove any residue. Place the sterilized lids on the jars and screw on the bands until fingertip-tight.

Process in a Water Bath:
- Process the jars in a boiling water bath for 15 minutes to ensure proper sealing.

Cool and Store:
- Allow the jars to cool completely. Check the seals by pressing down on the center of each lid. If it doesn't pop back, the jar is sealed.

Label and Store:
- Label the sealed jars with the date and store them in a cool, dark place.

Enjoy:
- Your tomato basil salsa is ready for use. Open a jar, and enjoy the flavors of summer all year long!

Tips:

- Follow proper canning procedures to ensure the safety and longevity of your preserved salsa.
- Adjust the spiciness by adding or omitting crushed red pepper flakes.
- Make sure to use ripe, high-quality tomatoes for the best flavor.

Desserts:

Apple Crisp with Oat Topping

Ingredients:

For the Apple Filling:

- 6 cups apples, peeled, cored, and sliced (a mix of sweet and tart varieties)
- 1/4 cup granulated sugar
- 1 tablespoon all-purpose flour
- 1 teaspoon ground cinnamon
- 1/4 teaspoon ground nutmeg
- 1 tablespoon lemon juice

For the Oat Topping:

- 1 cup old-fashioned rolled oats
- 1/2 cup all-purpose flour
- 1/2 cup brown sugar, packed
- 1/2 teaspoon ground cinnamon
- 1/4 teaspoon salt
- 1/2 cup unsalted butter, cold and diced

Instructions:

Preheat the Oven:
- Preheat your oven to 350°F (175°C).

Prepare the Apple Filling:
- In a large bowl, combine the sliced apples with granulated sugar, flour, ground cinnamon, ground nutmeg, and lemon juice. Toss until the apples are evenly coated.

Transfer to Baking Dish:
- Transfer the coated apples to a greased 9x13-inch baking dish or a similar-sized baking dish.

Prepare the Oat Topping:

- In a separate bowl, combine rolled oats, flour, brown sugar, ground cinnamon, and salt. Mix well.
- Add the cold, diced butter to the oat mixture. Using your fingers or a pastry cutter, work the butter into the dry ingredients until the mixture resembles coarse crumbs.

Assemble and Bake:
- Sprinkle the oat topping evenly over the apple filling in the baking dish.
- Bake in the preheated oven for 40-45 minutes or until the apple filling is bubbly, and the topping is golden brown and crisp.

Cool Slightly:
- Allow the apple crisp to cool for a few minutes before serving.

Serve:
- Serve warm, and optionally, with a scoop of vanilla ice cream or a dollop of whipped cream.

Enjoy:
- Enjoy your delicious Apple Crisp with Oat Topping!

Tips:

- You can mix different types of apples for a more complex flavor profile.
- Experiment with adding a handful of chopped nuts, such as pecans or walnuts, to the oat topping for extra crunch.
- Store any leftovers in the refrigerator and reheat before serving for a tasty treat on subsequent days.

Vegan Chocolate Avocado Mousse

Ingredients:

- 2 ripe avocados
- 1/2 cup cocoa powder (unsweetened)
- 1/2 cup maple syrup or agave nectar
- 1/4 cup coconut milk or any plant-based milk
- 1 teaspoon vanilla extract
- A pinch of salt
- Optional toppings: fresh berries, chopped nuts, shredded coconut

Instructions:

Prepare the Avocados:
- Cut the avocados in half, remove the pits, and scoop out the flesh into a blender or food processor.

Blend the Ingredients:
- Add cocoa powder, maple syrup or agave nectar, coconut milk, vanilla extract, and a pinch of salt to the blender or food processor.
- Blend until the mixture is smooth and creamy. You may need to stop and scrape down the sides to ensure everything is well incorporated.

Adjust Sweetness:
- Taste the mousse and adjust the sweetness if needed by adding more maple syrup or agave nectar.

Chill the Mousse:
- Transfer the chocolate avocado mixture into individual serving glasses or a larger bowl.
- Refrigerate the mousse for at least 2 hours to allow it to chill and set.

Serve:
- Once chilled, serve the Vegan Chocolate Avocado Mousse on its own or with your favorite toppings.

Optional Toppings:
- Garnish with fresh berries, chopped nuts, or shredded coconut before serving.

Enjoy:
- Enjoy this rich and creamy vegan dessert guilt-free!

Tips:

- Ensure the avocados are ripe for a smoother consistency.
- Adjust the sweetness to your liking by gradually adding the sweetener and tasting as you go.
- Feel free to experiment with additional flavors such as a hint of mint extract or a sprinkle of sea salt for a unique twist.
- This mousse is best served chilled but can be enjoyed immediately if you can't wait!

Coconut Mango Sorbet

Ingredients:

- 3 cups ripe mango, peeled, pitted, and diced (about 3 medium-sized mangoes)
- 1 can (13.5 oz) coconut milk (full-fat for creamier sorbet)
- 1/2 cup granulated sugar (adjust according to sweetness preference)
- 1 tablespoon lime or lemon juice
- Pinch of salt

Instructions:

Prepare the Mango:
- Peel, pit, and dice the ripe mangoes until you have about 3 cups.

Blend Ingredients:
- In a blender or food processor, combine the diced mango, coconut milk, granulated sugar, lime or lemon juice, and a pinch of salt.
- Blend until the mixture is smooth and well combined.

Taste and Adjust:
- Taste the mixture and adjust the sweetness or acidity by adding more sugar or lime/lemon juice if needed.

Chill the Mixture:
- Refrigerate the mixture for at least 2 hours to chill it thoroughly. This step enhances the flavor and helps the sorbet freeze more efficiently.

Churn the Sorbet:
- Pour the chilled mixture into an ice cream maker and churn according to the manufacturer's instructions. This usually takes about 20-25 minutes.

Transfer to a Container:
- Once the sorbet reaches a soft-serve consistency, transfer it to a lidded container.

Freeze:
- Freeze the sorbet for an additional 3-4 hours or until firm.

Serve:
- Scoop the Coconut Mango Sorbet into bowls or cones and enjoy!

Tips:

- If you don't have an ice cream maker, you can pour the mixture into a shallow dish, freeze for 1-2 hours, and then stir with a fork every 30 minutes until it reaches the desired consistency.
- Add shredded coconut or a splash of coconut rum for an extra layer of flavor.
- Garnish with fresh mint or additional mango slices when serving for a beautiful presentation.

Homemade Beverages:

Cucumber Mint Infused Water

Ingredients:

- 1 cucumber, thinly sliced
- A handful of fresh mint leaves
- 1 lemon, thinly sliced (optional)
- Ice cubes
- Water

Instructions:

Prepare the Ingredients:
- Wash the cucumber, mint leaves, and lemon (if using) thoroughly.

Slice the Cucumber:
- Cut the cucumber into thin slices. If the cucumber is organic, you can leave the skin on for added flavor.

Crush the Mint:
- Gently crush the mint leaves with your hands or a muddler. This helps release their natural oils and enhances the flavor.

Slice the Lemon (Optional):
- If using lemon, thinly slice it. You can also squeeze some lemon juice into the water for an extra citrusy kick.

Assemble the Infused Water:
- In a large pitcher, combine the cucumber slices, crushed mint leaves, lemon slices (if using), and ice cubes.

Add Water:
- Fill the pitcher with water. Use filtered or still water for the best taste.

Stir and Refrigerate:
- Give the infused water a gentle stir to mix the ingredients.
- Refrigerate the pitcher for at least 1-2 hours to allow the flavors to infuse.

Serve:
- Pour the cucumber mint infused water into glasses, and feel free to add more ice if desired.

Enjoy:
- Enjoy this refreshing and hydrating cucumber mint infused water, a perfect beverage for hot days or as a healthy alternative to sugary drinks.

Tips:

- Adjust the intensity of flavors by adding more or fewer cucumber slices, mint leaves, or lemon.
- For a sparkling version, use carbonated water instead of still water.
- Infused water is best consumed within 24 hours for optimal freshness and flavor.

Berry and Basil Lemonade

Ingredients:

- 1 cup mixed berries (strawberries, blueberries, raspberries)
- 1/4 cup fresh basil leaves
- 1 cup freshly squeezed lemon juice (about 4-6 lemons)
- 1/2 cup granulated sugar (adjust to taste)
- 4 cups cold water
- Ice cubes
- Lemon slices and fresh berries for garnish (optional)
- Basil leaves for garnish (optional)

Instructions:

Prepare the Berries and Basil:
- Wash and hull the berries. If using strawberries, slice them into halves or quarters.
- Wash the basil leaves and gently bruise them to release their flavor.

Make the Lemonade Base:
- In a blender, combine the mixed berries, basil leaves, and a splash of water. Blend until you have a smooth puree.
- Strain the berry-basil puree through a fine mesh sieve into a pitcher to remove any seeds and pulp.

Prepare the Lemonade:
- In the pitcher with the strained puree, add freshly squeezed lemon juice and granulated sugar. Stir until the sugar dissolves.
- Add cold water to the pitcher and mix well.

Taste and Adjust:
- Taste the lemonade and adjust the sweetness by adding more sugar if needed.

Chill:
- Refrigerate the lemonade for at least 1-2 hours to allow the flavors to meld and the mixture to chill.

Serve:
- Fill glasses with ice cubes and pour the berry and basil lemonade over the ice.

Garnish (Optional):

- Garnish with lemon slices, fresh berries, and additional basil leaves if desired.

Enjoy:
- Stir and enjoy the refreshing Berry and Basil Lemonade on a hot day!

Tips:

- You can customize the berry combination based on your preferences.
- Adjust the sweetness and tartness by modifying the amount of sugar and lemon juice.
- For a sparkling version, you can add soda water or sparkling water to the lemonade just before serving.

Iced Green Tea with Honey and Ginger

Ingredients:

- 4-5 green tea bags
- 1 tablespoon fresh ginger, grated or sliced
- 3-4 tablespoons honey (adjust to taste)
- Ice cubes
- Lemon slices for garnish (optional)
- Fresh mint leaves for garnish (optional)

Instructions:

Brew the Green Tea:
- Bring 4 cups of water to a boil. Once boiling, remove it from heat and add the green tea bags and grated or sliced ginger.
- Let the tea steep for 3-5 minutes, depending on your desired strength.

Sweeten with Honey:
- After steeping, remove the tea bags and stir in honey while the tea is still warm. Adjust the amount of honey to suit your sweetness preference.

Cool the Tea:
- Allow the tea to cool to room temperature. You can speed up the process by placing the pot in the refrigerator.

Refrigerate:
- Once the tea is at room temperature, transfer it to the refrigerator and let it chill for at least 1-2 hours.

Serve Over Ice:
- Fill glasses with ice cubes and pour the chilled green tea over the ice.

Garnish (Optional):
- Garnish the iced green tea with lemon slices and fresh mint leaves for a burst of freshness.

Stir and Enjoy:
- Stir the iced green tea well, and enjoy this refreshing and soothing beverage.

Tips:

- You can experiment with different types of green tea, such as sencha or jasmine green tea, to vary the flavor profile.

- Adjust the amount of ginger and honey to your taste preferences.
- To make it a sparkling iced tea, top off the chilled green tea with sparkling water just before serving.
- Make a larger batch and store it in the refrigerator for a convenient and refreshing drink throughout the day.

Fermented Foods:

Kimchi with Napa Cabbage

Ingredients:

- 1 large Napa cabbage
- 1/2 cup sea salt
- 3 cups water (for brining)
- 1 daikon radish, peeled and julienned
- 4 carrots, peeled and julienned
- 5 green onions, chopped
- 1 tablespoon ginger, grated
- 3 cloves garlic, minced
- 1 tablespoon sugar
- 3 tablespoons fish sauce or soy sauce for a vegan version
- 2-3 tablespoons Korean red pepper flakes (Gochugaru) or to taste

Instructions:

Prepare the Cabbage:
- Cut the Napa cabbage in half lengthwise and then into quarters. Remove the core.
- Dissolve the sea salt in water to create a brine. Soak the cabbage quarters in the brine, making sure to get the salt between the leaves. Let it sit for 1-2 hours, turning occasionally.

Rinse and Drain:
- After brining, rinse the cabbage quarters under cold water to remove excess salt. Drain them in a colander for about 30 minutes.

Prepare the Vegetables:
- While the cabbage is draining, julienne the daikon radish and carrots, chop the green onions, and grate the ginger.

Make the Kimchi Paste:
- In a large bowl, combine the daikon radish, carrots, green onions, ginger, garlic, sugar, fish sauce or soy sauce, and Korean red pepper flakes. Mix well to create a paste.

Cut and Mix with Cabbage:

- Cut the drained cabbage quarters into bite-sized pieces. Add the cabbage to the paste, wearing gloves to protect your hands from the red pepper flakes. Mix thoroughly, ensuring the cabbage is well coated.

Pack into Jars:
- Pack the kimchi mixture into clean, airtight jars, pressing it down to remove air pockets. Leave some space at the top to allow for expansion during fermentation.

Fermentation:
- Seal the jars and let them sit at room temperature for 1-5 days, depending on your desired level of fermentation. Check daily, pressing down on the kimchi to submerge it in its juices.

Refrigerate:
- Once the kimchi reaches your preferred level of fermentation, move the jars to the refrigerator to slow down the fermentation process.

Serve:
- Kimchi is ready to be served! Enjoy it as a side dish, in sandwiches, or as an ingredient in various recipes.

Tips:

- The fermentation time depends on your taste preference. Taste the kimchi daily, and when it reaches the desired flavor, refrigerate to halt the fermentation process.
- Use non-reactive utensils and containers (plastic, glass, or stainless steel) as reactive materials can affect the fermentation process.

Homemade Sauerkraut with Caraway Seeds

Ingredients:

- 1 medium-sized green cabbage (about 2-3 pounds)
- 1 tablespoon sea salt (non-iodized)
- 1 tablespoon caraway seeds

Equipment:

- A large mixing bowl
- Clean glass jars or a fermentation crock
- A weight (like a smaller jar or a sterilized stone)
- Cheesecloth or a clean kitchen towel
- Rubber bands or string

Instructions:

Prepare the Cabbage:
- Remove the outer leaves of the cabbage and set them aside. Quarter the cabbage and remove the core. Thinly slice the cabbage into shreds.

Massage with Salt:
- Place the shredded cabbage in a large mixing bowl and sprinkle the sea salt over it. Begin massaging the cabbage with your hands, breaking down its cell walls and allowing it to release its juices. This process can take about 5-10 minutes.

Add Caraway Seeds:
- Once the cabbage has released enough liquid, add caraway seeds and mix them into the cabbage.

Pack into Jars or Crock:
- Pack the salted and seeded cabbage into clean glass jars or a fermentation crock. Press it down firmly to remove air pockets and ensure the cabbage is submerged in its juices.

Use the Outer Leaves:
- Take the outer leaves you set aside earlier and place them on top of the shredded cabbage to act as a natural weight. This helps keep the cabbage submerged in its own juices.

Weigh Down the Cabbage:

- Place a weight (a smaller jar or sterilized stone) on top of the cabbage to keep it submerged. This is important for the fermentation process.

Cover and Secure:
- Cover the jars or crock with a cheesecloth or clean kitchen towel and secure it with rubber bands or string. This allows air circulation while preventing debris from entering.

Fermentation:
- Allow the sauerkraut to ferment at room temperature (ideally between 65-75°F or 18-24°C) for 1-4 weeks, depending on your desired level of fermentation. Check regularly and press the cabbage down to release gases.

Taste and Refrigerate:
- Taste the sauerkraut after a week and continue fermenting until it reaches your preferred flavor. Once satisfied, remove the outer leaves, weight, and cheesecloth. Seal with a lid and refrigerate.

Serve:
- Your homemade sauerkraut with caraway seeds is ready to be served as a flavorful condiment or side dish.

Tips:

- Use clean and sterilized equipment to avoid unwanted bacteria interfering with the fermentation process.
- Experiment with the amount of caraway seeds according to your taste preference.
- Always make sure the cabbage is submerged in its juices to prevent mold formation. If needed, you can add a bit of brine (saltwater solution) to cover the cabbage.

Pickled Jalapeños for Toppings

Ingredients:

- 1 pound fresh jalapeños, sliced (about 2-3 cups)
- 1 cup white vinegar
- 1 cup water
- 2 tablespoons sugar
- 1 tablespoon salt
- 2 cloves garlic, peeled and lightly crushed (optional)

Instructions:

Prepare the Jalapeños:
- Wash the jalapeños thoroughly. Wear gloves while handling them, especially if you have sensitive skin or are sensitive to spicy foods.
- Slice the jalapeños into rounds or strips, depending on your preference. Remove the seeds for a milder flavor or leave them in for extra heat.

Prepare the Pickling Liquid:
- In a saucepan, combine white vinegar, water, sugar, salt, and crushed garlic cloves. Bring the mixture to a boil over medium-high heat, stirring to dissolve the sugar and salt.

Pack the Jars:
- Pack the sliced jalapeños into clean, sterile jars. If you like, you can add a garlic clove or two into each jar for added flavor.

Pour the Pickling Liquid:
- Pour the hot pickling liquid over the jalapeños in the jars, ensuring they are completely submerged. Leave about 1/2-inch headspace at the top of the jars.

Remove Air Bubbles:
- Gently tap the jars on the counter to remove any air bubbles. If necessary, use a clean utensil to release trapped air.

Seal the Jars:
- Wipe the rims of the jars with a clean, damp cloth to remove any residue. Place the sterilized lids on the jars and screw on the bands until fingertip-tight.

Cool and Store:

- Allow the jars to cool to room temperature. Once cooled, move them to the refrigerator.

Wait and Enjoy:
- Let the pickled jalapeños sit in the refrigerator for at least 24 hours before using to allow the flavors to meld.

Serve:
- Use your homemade pickled jalapeños as a topping for tacos, burgers, sandwiches, nachos, or any dish that could use a spicy kick.

Tips:

- Adjust the sugar and salt quantities to suit your taste preferences.
- Experiment with adding other spices like cumin seeds, coriander seeds, or black peppercorns for additional flavor.
- Pickled jalapeños can be stored in the refrigerator for several weeks.

Global Flavors:

Thai-Inspired Pineapple Fried Rice

Ingredients:

- 2 cups cooked jasmine rice (preferably cooled or day-old rice)
- 1 cup pineapple chunks, fresh or canned
- 1 cup mixed vegetables (peas, carrots, corn, bell peppers), diced
- 1/2 cup tofu or cooked chicken, diced (optional)
- 3 tablespoons vegetable oil
- 3 cloves garlic, minced
- 1 shallot, finely chopped
- 2 green onions, sliced
- 1/4 cup cashews or peanuts, chopped
- 2 eggs, beaten
- 3 tablespoons soy sauce
- 1 tablespoon fish sauce or soy sauce for a vegetarian version
- 1 tablespoon curry powder
- 1/2 teaspoon turmeric powder (optional, for color)
- Fresh cilantro for garnish (optional)
- Lime wedges for serving

Instructions:

Prepare Ingredients:
- Cook jasmine rice according to package instructions. For the best results, use cooled or day-old rice.
- If using fresh pineapple, peel and dice it into small chunks. If using canned pineapple, drain the juice.
- Dice the mixed vegetables, tofu or chicken, garlic, shallot, and green onions.

Stir-Fry Vegetables:
- Heat 2 tablespoons of vegetable oil in a large wok or skillet over medium-high heat. Add garlic and shallot, and stir-fry for about 1 minute until fragrant.
- Add mixed vegetables and cook for 2-3 minutes until they start to soften.

Add Tofu or Chicken (Optional):

- Push the vegetables to one side of the wok and add the remaining oil. If using tofu or chicken, cook until browned and cooked through.

Scramble Eggs:
- Push the vegetables and protein to the side and pour the beaten eggs into the empty space. Scramble the eggs until cooked.

Combine Ingredients:
- Mix everything together in the wok, including the cooked rice. Stir well to combine all the ingredients.

Add Pineapple and Nuts:
- Add pineapple chunks and chopped cashews or peanuts. Continue to stir-fry for another 2-3 minutes.

Season the Fried Rice:
- In a small bowl, mix soy sauce, fish sauce (or additional soy sauce for a vegetarian version), and curry powder. Pour the sauce over the rice mixture and stir to coat evenly.
- Add turmeric powder for a golden color if desired.

Finish and Garnish:
- Stir in sliced green onions and cook for an additional minute. Taste and adjust the seasoning if needed.
- Garnish with fresh cilantro if desired.

Serve:
- Serve the Thai-Inspired Pineapple Fried Rice hot, with lime wedges on the side for squeezing.

Enjoy your delicious and vibrant pineapple fried rice!

Mediterranean Chickpea Salad with Feta

Ingredients:

- 2 cans (15 ounces each) chickpeas, drained and rinsed
- 1 cup cherry tomatoes, halved
- 1 cucumber, diced
- 1 red bell pepper, diced
- 1/2 red onion, finely chopped
- 1/2 cup Kalamata olives, pitted and sliced
- 1/2 cup crumbled feta cheese
- 1/4 cup fresh parsley, chopped
- 1/4 cup extra-virgin olive oil
- 2 tablespoons red wine vinegar
- 1 teaspoon dried oregano
- Salt and pepper to taste
- Lemon wedges for serving (optional)

Instructions:

Prepare the Chickpeas:
- Drain and rinse the chickpeas thoroughly under cold water.

Chop Vegetables:
- In a large bowl, combine the halved cherry tomatoes, diced cucumber, diced red bell pepper, finely chopped red onion, sliced Kalamata olives, and chopped fresh parsley.

Add Chickpeas:
- Add the drained and rinsed chickpeas to the bowl with the vegetables.

Make the Dressing:
- In a small bowl, whisk together the extra-virgin olive oil, red wine vinegar, dried oregano, salt, and pepper.

Assemble the Salad:
- Pour the dressing over the chickpea and vegetable mixture. Toss everything together until well combined.

Add Feta:
- Gently fold in the crumbled feta cheese. Adjust the seasoning if needed.

Chill:
- Cover the bowl and refrigerate the chickpea salad for at least 30 minutes to allow the flavors to meld.

Serve:
- Before serving, give the salad a final toss. Serve the Mediterranean Chickpea Salad with Feta chilled.

Optional:
- Serve with lemon wedges on the side for an extra burst of citrus flavor.

Enjoy this flavorful and nutritious Mediterranean Chickpea Salad as a light lunch, a side dish, or a refreshing addition to your summer menu!

Mexican Quinoa Stuffed Peppers

Ingredients:

- 4 large bell peppers, any color
- 1 cup quinoa, rinsed
- 2 cups vegetable broth or water
- 1 tablespoon olive oil
- 1 onion, diced
- 2 cloves garlic, minced
- 1 can (15 ounces) black beans, drained and rinsed
- 1 cup corn kernels (fresh, frozen, or canned)
- 1 cup diced tomatoes
- 1 teaspoon ground cumin
- 1 teaspoon chili powder
- 1/2 teaspoon paprika
- Salt and pepper to taste
- 1 cup shredded Mexican cheese blend
- Fresh cilantro, chopped, for garnish (optional)
- Avocado slices for serving (optional)
- Lime wedges for serving (optional)

Instructions:

Preheat the Oven:
- Preheat your oven to 375°F (190°C).

Prepare the Quinoa:
- In a medium saucepan, combine quinoa and vegetable broth (or water). Bring to a boil, then reduce heat to low, cover, and simmer for 15-20 minutes or until the quinoa is cooked and the liquid is absorbed.

Prepare the Bell Peppers:
- Cut the tops off the bell peppers, remove the seeds and membranes, and lightly brush them with olive oil. Place them in a baking dish.

Saute the Onion and Garlic:
- In a large skillet, heat olive oil over medium heat. Add diced onion and sauté until translucent. Add minced garlic and cook for an additional 1-2 minutes.

Combine Ingredients:

- To the skillet, add cooked quinoa, black beans, corn, diced tomatoes, ground cumin, chili powder, paprika, salt, and pepper. Stir to combine.

Stuff the Peppers:
- Stuff each bell pepper with the quinoa mixture, pressing it down gently. Top each stuffed pepper with shredded Mexican cheese.

Bake:
- Cover the baking dish with aluminum foil and bake in the preheated oven for 25-30 minutes or until the peppers are tender.

Garnish and Serve:
- Remove from the oven and garnish with chopped cilantro if desired. Serve the Mexican Quinoa Stuffed Peppers with avocado slices and lime wedges on the side.

Enjoy these flavorful and wholesome stuffed peppers as a satisfying main dish!

Hearty Bowls:

Soba Noodle Buddha Bowl with Sesame Ginger Dressing

Ingredients:

For the Buddha Bowl:

- 8 oz (about 225g) soba noodles
- 1 cup shredded purple cabbage
- 1 cup shredded carrots
- 1 cup cucumber, julienned
- 1 cup edamame, cooked
- 1 avocado, sliced
- 1 cup red bell pepper, thinly sliced
- 1/4 cup green onions, sliced
- Sesame seeds for garnish
- Chopped cilantro for garnish

For the Sesame Ginger Dressing:

- 3 tablespoons soy sauce
- 2 tablespoons rice vinegar
- 1 tablespoon sesame oil
- 1 tablespoon fresh ginger, grated
- 1 clove garlic, minced
- 1 tablespoon honey or maple syrup for a vegan version
- 2 tablespoons neutral oil (such as vegetable or grapeseed oil)
- 1 tablespoon sesame seeds (optional)

Instructions:

Cook the Soba Noodles:
- Cook the soba noodles according to the package instructions. Once cooked, drain and rinse under cold water to stop the cooking process. Set aside.

Prepare the Vegetables:
- Shred the purple cabbage, carrots, and thinly slice the cucumber and red bell pepper. Cook edamame if not already cooked.

Assemble the Buddha Bowl:
- In serving bowls, arrange a portion of soba noodles and top with shredded cabbage, carrots, cucumber, edamame, avocado slices, and red bell pepper.

Make the Sesame Ginger Dressing:
- In a small bowl, whisk together soy sauce, rice vinegar, sesame oil, grated ginger, minced garlic, honey or maple syrup, neutral oil, and sesame seeds if using.

Drizzle the Dressing:
- Drizzle the Sesame Ginger Dressing over the assembled Buddha bowls.

Garnish:
- Garnish the bowls with sliced green onions, sesame seeds, and chopped cilantro.

Serve:
- Serve the Soba Noodle Buddha Bowl immediately and enjoy!

Feel free to customize the Buddha bowl with your favorite vegetables or proteins like tofu, grilled chicken, or shrimp. This vibrant and flavorful bowl makes for a satisfying and healthy meal.

Moroccan Spiced Couscous Bowl with Roasted Vegetables

Ingredients:

For the Roasted Vegetables:

- 1 eggplant, diced
- 2 zucchini, sliced
- 1 red bell pepper, chopped
- 1 red onion, sliced
- 2 tablespoons olive oil
- 1 teaspoon ground cumin
- 1 teaspoon ground coriander
- 1 teaspoon smoked paprika
- Salt and pepper to taste

For the Couscous:

- 1 cup couscous
- 1 1/4 cups vegetable broth or water
- 1 tablespoon olive oil
- 1 teaspoon ground cumin
- 1 teaspoon ground coriander
- 1/2 teaspoon ground cinnamon
- Salt and pepper to taste

For the Yogurt Sauce:

- 1/2 cup Greek yogurt
- 1 tablespoon fresh lemon juice
- 1 tablespoon fresh mint, chopped
- Salt and pepper to taste

Optional Garnishes:

- Chopped fresh cilantro or parsley
- Pomegranate seeds
- Sliced almonds or pine nuts, toasted

Instructions:

Preheat the Oven:
- Preheat your oven to 400°F (200°C).

Prepare the Roasted Vegetables:
- In a large mixing bowl, combine the diced eggplant, sliced zucchini, chopped red bell pepper, and sliced red onion. Drizzle with olive oil and sprinkle with ground cumin, ground coriander, smoked paprika, salt, and pepper. Toss to coat the vegetables evenly.
- Spread the seasoned vegetables on a baking sheet in a single layer. Roast in the preheated oven for 25-30 minutes or until they are tender and slightly caramelized, stirring halfway through.

Cook the Couscous:
- In a saucepan, bring the vegetable broth or water to a boil. Stir in couscous, cover, and remove from heat. Let it sit for 5 minutes, then fluff the couscous with a fork.
- In a separate pan, heat olive oil over medium heat. Add ground cumin, ground coriander, ground cinnamon, salt, and pepper. Cook for a minute until the spices are fragrant.
- Add the cooked couscous to the pan with the spices and toss to coat evenly.

Prepare the Yogurt Sauce:
- In a small bowl, mix Greek yogurt, fresh lemon juice, chopped mint, salt, and pepper. Stir until well combined.

Assemble the Bowl:
- Divide the spiced couscous among serving bowls. Top with the roasted vegetables.

Drizzle with Yogurt Sauce:
- Drizzle the yogurt sauce over the couscous and vegetables.

Garnish:
- Garnish the bowl with optional toppings such as chopped fresh cilantro or parsley, pomegranate seeds, and toasted sliced almonds or pine nuts.

Serve:
- Serve the Moroccan Spiced Couscous Bowl warm and enjoy the rich and aromatic flavors!

This dish offers a delightful combination of textures and flavors, making it a satisfying and wholesome meal.

Teriyaki Tofu and Brown Rice Bowl

Ingredients:

For the Teriyaki Tofu:

- 1 block (14-16 ounces) extra-firm tofu, pressed and cubed
- 1/2 cup soy sauce
- 1/4 cup water
- 2 tablespoons rice vinegar
- 2 tablespoons brown sugar
- 2 cloves garlic, minced
- 1 teaspoon fresh ginger, grated
- 1 tablespoon cornstarch (optional, for thickening)
- 2 tablespoons vegetable oil, for cooking

For the Brown Rice Bowl:

- 2 cups cooked brown rice
- 1 cup broccoli florets, blanched
- 1 carrot, julienned or grated
- 1 red bell pepper, thinly sliced
- Sesame seeds for garnish
- Sliced green onions for garnish

Instructions:

Prepare the Teriyaki Tofu:
- In a bowl, whisk together soy sauce, water, rice vinegar, brown sugar, minced garlic, and grated ginger to make the teriyaki sauce. If you prefer a thicker sauce, mix in cornstarch.
- Press the tofu to remove excess water, then cut it into cubes.
- Heat vegetable oil in a pan over medium-high heat. Add tofu cubes and cook until they are golden brown on all sides.
- Pour the teriyaki sauce over the tofu cubes, stirring gently to coat. Simmer for a few minutes until the sauce thickens and coats the tofu.

Prepare the Brown Rice Bowl:

- Divide cooked brown rice among serving bowls.
- Arrange blanched broccoli florets, julienned or grated carrot, and sliced red bell pepper on top of the rice.

Top with Teriyaki Tofu:
- Spoon the teriyaki tofu over the vegetables and rice.

Garnish:
- Sprinkle sesame seeds and sliced green onions over the bowl for added flavor and texture.

Serve:
- Serve the Teriyaki Tofu and Brown Rice Bowl immediately, and enjoy the delicious combination of flavors and textures.

This Teriyaki Tofu and Brown Rice Bowl is a well-balanced and satisfying meal that's easy to prepare at home. Feel free to customize the vegetables and toppings based on your preferences.